Stunt Planes

By Jeff Savage

CAPSTONE
HIGH-INTEREST
BOOKS

an imprint of Capstone Press
Mankato, Minnesota

Capstone High-Interest Books are published by Capstone Press
151 Good Counsel Drive, P.O. Box 669, Mankato, Minnesota 56002
http://www.capstone-press.com

Library of Congress Cataloging-in-Publication Data
Savage, Jeff, 1961–
    Stunt planes/by Jeff Savage.
    p. cm.—(Wild rides!)
    Includes bibliographical references and index.
    Summary: Describes the sport of stunt flying, including its history, the
most popular stunt planes, basic stunts, and stunt flying contests.
    ISBN 0-7368-1519-8 (hardcover)
    1. Stunt flying—Juvenile literature. 2. Airplanes—Juvenile literature.
[1. Stunt flying. 2. Airplanes.] I. Title. II. Series.
TL711.S8 S28 2003
797.5'4—dc21   2002012576

**Capstone Press would like to thank Lt. Mike Blankenship of the
Blue Angels for his help in preparing this book.**

Editorial Credits
Matt Doeden, editor; Karen Risch, product planning editor; Kia Adams,
    series designer; Gene Bentdahl and Molly Nei, book designers;
    Jo Miller, photo researcher

Photo Credits
Corbis/Stephanie Maze, 10; Peter Turnley, 27
The Image Finders/T. A. Wagner, 7, 16
Photo by Ted Carlson/Fotodynamics, 4, 12, 15, 20, 22, 28
The Viesti Collection, Inc./Bill Gallery, 8–9; Walter Bibikow, 24–25
Wernher Krutein, cover
www.ronkimballstock.com, 19

1 2 3 4 5 6 08 07 06 05 04 03

Table of Contents

Learn about:

- Aerobatics

- Training

- Types of stunt planes

CHAPTER 1

4

Stunt Planes

Thousands of people gather along Lake Michigan in Chicago, Illinois, for an air show. They watch as four blue-and-yellow jets fly overhead. Together, the planes form the shape of a diamond. They fly very close. Their wings are only a few feet apart.

The planes zoom over the lake at a speed of 500 miles (805 kilometers) per hour. The sound of their powerful jet engines is louder than thunder.

The jets go into a steep climb. The pilots flip a switch that sends thick white smoke out the rear of the planes. Four white lines show the paths of the jets. The planes climb nearly 1 mile (1.6 kilometers) in a few seconds.

Suddenly, the four planes separate and fall away from each other. Each plane loops in a different direction. The pilots steer the planes into tight rolls as they curve back down toward the water. Each pilot pulls up at the last moment to avoid crashing into the lake. The crowd cheers as the pilots prepare to perform their next stunt.

About Stunt Planes

A stunt plane is any kind of airplane pilots use to perform tricks. These tricks are also called stunts or aerobatics. Few planes are built specially to perform aerobatics. Most stunt planes are designed for other purposes. Some are small-engine airplanes designed to carry people on short trips. Others are military jets built for combat and defense.

Stunt pilots usually perform aerobatics at air shows. Some air shows are small. These shows may include only a few planes that perform for several hundred people. The Chicago Air and Water Show and other large air shows include hundreds of planes that perform for 100,000 people or more.

Stunt pilots need a great deal of training. They first take basic flying lessons to earn a pilot's license. They then take special classes to learn aerobatics. Pilots must finally pass a series of flying tests before they can become stunt pilots.

Stunt pilots often fly upside down when they perform aerobatics.

Types of Stunt Planes

Stunt pilots can fly many kinds of planes. Any plane that is highly maneuverable can be a stunt plane. Most highly maneuverable planes are small. They can turn quickly. Stunt planes should also be sturdy. Stunts often place a great deal of stress on the plane's frame.

Propeller-driven planes are common stunt planes. These planes have at least one propeller. The propeller spins to force air over the wings and lift the plane. Two main kinds of

Stunt pilots can choose from many kinds of planes, including monoplanes and biplanes.

propeller-driven airplanes are used as stunt planes. Monoplanes have a single set of wings either above or below the cockpit. Biplanes have two sets of wings. One set is above the cockpit, and the other is below.

Jet airplanes also can be used as stunt planes. These airplanes are more powerful and much faster than propeller-driven airplanes. Only very experienced pilots should attempt stunts in jet airplanes.

Learn about:

- **The first stunts**

- **Barnstormers**

- **Today's stunt planes**

CHAPTER 2

Early Models of Stunt Planes

Pilots have been performing aerobatics for more than 90 years. In 1913, a Russian pilot named Peter Bestrov completed the first airplane loop. One month later, an American named Lincoln Beachey did the same trick. Soon, other pilots performed airplane stunts.

Airplanes were first used in combat during World War I (1914–1918). Pilots often avoided enemy gunfire by performing rolls and loops with their airplanes. These moves later became popular with stunt pilots.

The Stearman Model 75 was a popular stunt plane after World War II. People often used this plane to do a stunt called wing walking.

After the war, the U.S. military no longer needed all of its planes. Some pilots bought the used planes. They flew the planes to air shows around the United States. They performed tricks for

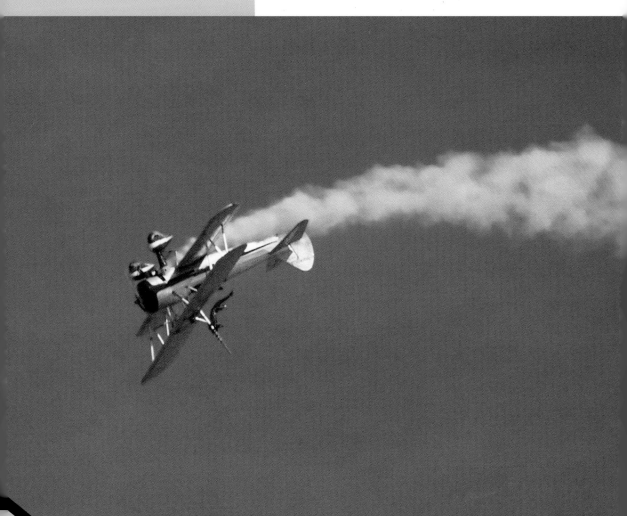

crowds and took people for rides. These pilots were called "barnstormers" because they often parked their planes next to barns.

Stunt Plane Models

The barnstormers used several models of warplanes. The most popular model was the Curtiss JN-4D. It was a type of biplane built by Glen Curtiss in 1914. Pilots called the plane the "Jenny." Another common stunt plane was the J-1. The U.S. military used the J-1 to train pilots for the war.

Many of the planes used in World War II (1939–1945) later became popular stunt planes. The Stearman Model 75 was the most popular of these planes. Pilots still use the Stearman in stunt performances today.

Some planes were built just for stunt flying. The first such plane was the Pitts Special. It was designed in 1942 by Curtis Pitts. The Pitts Special is a 15-foot-long (4.6-meter-long) biplane. In 1971, Frank Christensen designed the Christen Eagle as a stunt plane.

Today's Stunt Planes

Small biplanes and monoplanes are still popular stunt planes today. But the most famous modern stunt planes are jets. Two of the best stunt teams in the world are the U.S. Navy's Blue Angels and the U.S. Air Force's Thunderbirds.

The Navy formed the Blue Angels in 1946. The group has performed for more than 350 million people since then. The Blue Angels are best known for flying in a tight diamond pattern. Today, the Blue Angels fly Boeing F/A-18 Hornets. These attack jets can reach speeds of more than 1,300 miles (2,100 kilometers) per hour.

The Air Force formed the Thunderbirds in 1953. On July 4, 1987, the team performed for a crowd of more than 2 million people at Coney Island in New York. Today, the Thunderbirds fly Lockheed Martin F-16C Fighting Falcons. These jets can reach speeds of more than 1,500 miles (2,400 kilometers) per hour.

Military groups in other countries also have flight teams. The Canadian Air Force has a team called the Snowbirds. Great Britain's Royal Air Force has a team called the Red Arrows.

The Thunderbirds fly F-16C Fighting Falcons.

Learn about:

- Airplane design

- Basic controls

- Stunt plane features

CHAPTER **3**

Designing a Stunt Plane

Stunt planes can be many shapes and sizes. Some are only 13 feet (4 meters) long and weigh 600 pounds (272 kilograms). Other stunt planes are high-powered jets measuring more than 50 feet (15 meters) long and weighing 50,000 pounds (22,700 kilograms) or more.

Pilots and stunt teams perform stunts that work well with each type of plane. For example, small propeller-driven planes are good at doing loops and dives. Jets can easily do rolls and high-speed climbs.

Design and Instruments

A stunt plane is similar to a standard plane in most ways. The basic outer structure includes the fuselage, wings, and tail. The fuselage is the frame of the plane. All other main parts, including the wings and the tail, connect to the fuselage. The rudder sits at the end of the tail. The pilot controls the rudder to steer the plane.

A stunt plane has the same instruments as a standard plane. The air speed indicator shows how fast the plane is flying. The tachometer displays how hard the engine is working. The altimeter shows how high above the ground the plane is flying. The horizon indicator shows whether the plane is level or tilted. In an emergency, a pilot can fly the stunt plane just by looking at the instruments.

An instrument panel helps a stunt pilot fly a plane.

Trails of smoke show the paths that stunt planes have taken.

Special Features

Stunt planes must be sturdy. Aerobatics put stress on a plane's fuselage, wings, and tail. Many standard planes are not built to withstand the stress of aerobatics.

In standard airplanes, pilots often steer with a device that looks like a steering wheel. A stunt pilot often uses a control stick instead of a wheel. The control stick opens and closes wing flaps called ailerons and elevators. Ailerons are flaps near the wingtips that control the horizontal level of a plane. Elevators are flaps that control climbing and diving.

Stunt plane pilots sometimes release colorful trails of smoke. Some stunt planes have small tanks of colored oil under the fuselage at the back of the plane. The pilot pushes a button that pumps the oil into the exhaust nozzles. The heated air from the exhaust turns the oil into colorful smoke. This smoke shows the path of the stunt plane.

Learn about:

- **Formations**

- **Loops and rolls**

- **Safety**

CHAPTER 4

Stunt Planes in Flight

Stunt pilots often travel around the world to take part in air shows. They may perform solo shows or in teams with many other planes. Teams often fly in groups called formations. Common formation shapes include the diamond, line, and square.

Some stunt teams have their own announcers. These team members explain the team's stunts to the people watching the show. The announcers also talk about the planes and the training that the pilots must have to join the team.

Maneuvers

Stunt pilots perform many aerobatics, but most pilots start with a few basic moves. Flying "inverted" is one of the most basic stunts. Pilots fly upside down for a short period of time. They cannot fly inverted for long, because they can pass out easily.

The loop is another basic stunt. From a level position, the pilot pulls the plane into a steep climb. The plane then makes a full circle in the air. The pilot is inverted for a moment before the plane levels out again.

Pilots also perform rolls. Rolls begin with the plane flying level. The pilot then drops one wing so the plane is no longer level. The plane spins into an inverted position before returning to a level position.

Pilots combine basic aerobatics to create more difficult stunts. For example, a pilot may perform a loop and a roll at the same time. Two pilots may fly toward one another, then perform rolls at the same time to avoid a crash. Only highly experienced stunt pilots should attempt these dangerous stunts.

Pilots begin loops by pulling into a steep climb.

Safety

Stunt flying is dangerous. Pilots must have a great deal of flight training before they attempt aerobatics. They should be careful never to try stunts that are too advanced for their skill level.

The weather must meet several conditions before stunt flying is safe. Clouds should be no lower than 1,500 feet (457 meters) above the ground. The pilot should be able to see at least 3 miles (4.8 kilometers) in every direction. Pilots should not attempt stunts in rainy or snowy weather.

Pilots also must carefully examine their planes before performing aerobatics. This examination is called the preflight inspection. Pilots must be certain that their planes are in perfect working condition.

Safety equipment also helps keep pilots safe. Pilots wear helmets and flight suits for protection. They are strapped to their seats with harnesses. The harnesses include five straps that go over the shoulders, around the waist, and between the legs.

No amount of safety features can make stunt flying completely safe. Pilots know their sport is dangerous. They believe the excitement of stunt flying is worth the risks.

Stunt pilots wear helmets and flight suits for protection.

The Blue Angels

The U.S. Navy's Blue Angels are one of the most famous flight teams in history. Six Navy pilots and their support team travel around the world to perform in air shows. The Blue Angels perform in about 70 shows each year between March and November.

The Blue Angels fly F/A-18 Hornets. The Navy first used these fighter jets in the early 1980s. The Blue Angels' Hornets are different from standard Navy Hornets. They do not have weapons. They also have a different paint job. Blue Angels' Hornets are painted blue with gold trim. Blue and gold are the Navy's official colors.

To join the Blue Angels, a pilot must have at least 1,350 hours of experience in a fighter plane. Most pilots have at least 10 years of Navy service. Once selected, pilots can remain on the team for only two years.

Words to Know

aerobatics (air-uh-BAT-iks)—stunts performed in the air

aileron (AY-luh-ron)—flaps near a plane's wingtips that control the horizontal level of the plane

biplane (BYE-plane)—an airplane with two sets of wings

cockpit (KOK-pit)—the area in the front of a plane where the pilot sits

formation (for-MAY-shuhn)—a group of airplanes flying together in a pattern

fuselage (FYOO-suh-lahzh)—the main body of an airplane

inverted (in-VUR-tuhd)—upside down

monoplane (MON-uh-plane)—an airplane with one set of wings

propeller (pruh-PEL-ur)—a set of rotating blades that provide the force to move an airplane through the air

To Learn More

Bledsoe, Glen, and Karen Bledsoe. *The Blue Angels: The U.S. Navy Flight Demonstration Squadron.* Serving Your Country. Mankato, Minn.: Capstone Press, 2001.

Gaffney, Timothy R. *Air Show Pilots and Airplanes.* Aircraft. Berkeley Heights, N.J.: Enslow Publishers, 2001.

Hopkins, Ellen. *The Thunderbirds: The U.S. Air Force Aerial Demonstration Squadron.* Serving Your Country. Mankato, Minn.: Capstone Press, 2001.

Useful Addresses

Canadian Air Force Snowbirds
431 (AD) Sqn
15 Wing
P.O. Box 5000
Moose Jaw, SK S6H 7Z8
Canada

U.S. Navy Blue Angels
Blue Angels Public Affairs Office
390 San Carlos Road, Suite A
Pensacola, FL 32508-5508

Internet Sites

Track down many sites about Stunt Planes.
Visit the FACT HOUND at *http://www.facthound.com*

IT IS EASY! IT IS FUN!

1) Go to *http://www.facthound.com*
2) Type in: 0736815198
3) Click on "FETCH IT" and FACT HOUND will find
   several links hand-picked by our editors.

Relax and let our pal FACT HOUND do the research for you!

Index